A Let's-Read-and-Find-Out Book™

# LOOK AT YOUR EYES

by PAUL SHOWERS • illustrated by TRUE KELLEY

Revised Edition

**HarperTrophy**

*A Division of HarperCollins Publishers*

Library of Congress Cataloging-in-Publication Data
Showers, Paul.
    Look at your eyes / by Paul Showers ; illustrated by True Kelley. —
Rev. ed.
        p.       cm. — (A Let's-read-and-find-out book)
    Summary: Describes the parts of the eye and how they work.
    ISBN 0-06-445108-9. (pbk.)
    1. Eye—Physiology—Juvenile literature.    2. Vision—Juvenile
literature. [1. Eye.    2. Vision.    3. Senses and sensation.]
I. Kelley, True, ill.    II. Title.
QP475.7.S53    1992b                                91-10168
612.8'4—dc20                                             CIP
                                                         AC

Published in hardcover by HarperCollins Publishers.
First Harper Trophy edition, 1992.

# LOOK AT YOUR EYES

When I get up in the morning, I go to the bathroom, and I wash my face and brush my teeth.

I look at my teeth in the mirror. Sometimes I make faces. I frown and make my eyes look fierce. I smile and make my eyes look happy. Sometimes I just try to look goofy.

It's fun to look in the mirror. I like to watch my eyes. My eyes are looking at my eyes. What do they see?

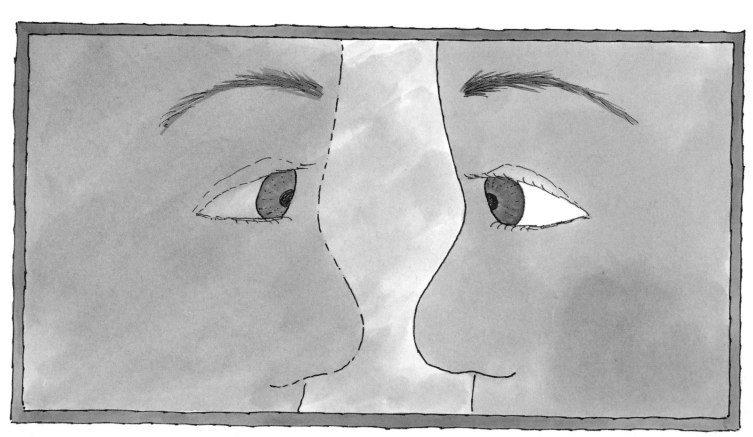

10

They see the color. My eyes are brown. So are my father's. My mother's eyes are hazel. Aunt Ruth's eyes are blue. Uncle Ned's eyes are green. What color are your eyes?

There are eyebrows over my eyes. There are eyelashes
around my eyes. My eyebrows and eyelashes are made up
of little hairs.

I have eyelids, too. They close down over my eyes when
I blink. They stay closed when I go to sleep.

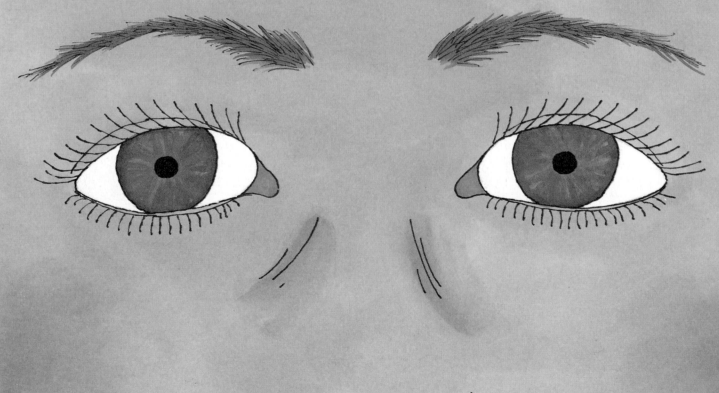

Aunt Ruth says eyebrows and eyelashes help to keep dust from falling into your eyes. Eyelids do the same thing and keep your eyes moist at all times. Aunt Ruth is a doctor. She tells me a lot of things about my eyes.

Your eyes can move in all directions—up, down, from one side to the other.

You can't watch your eyes when they move. But there is a way to see how they move.

Look straight at your eyes in the mirror. Keep looking straight and turn your head to one side. Turn it to the other. When you turn your head, your eyes move from side to side.

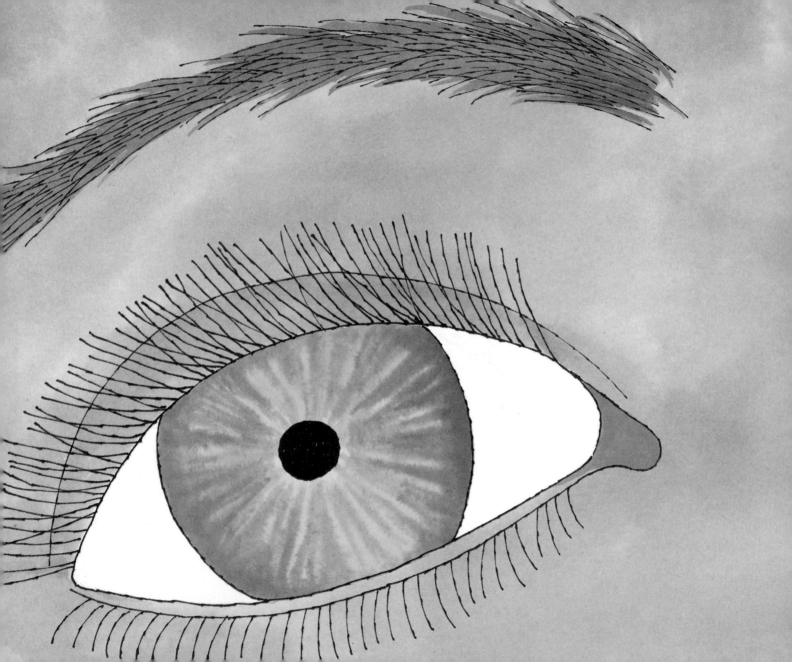

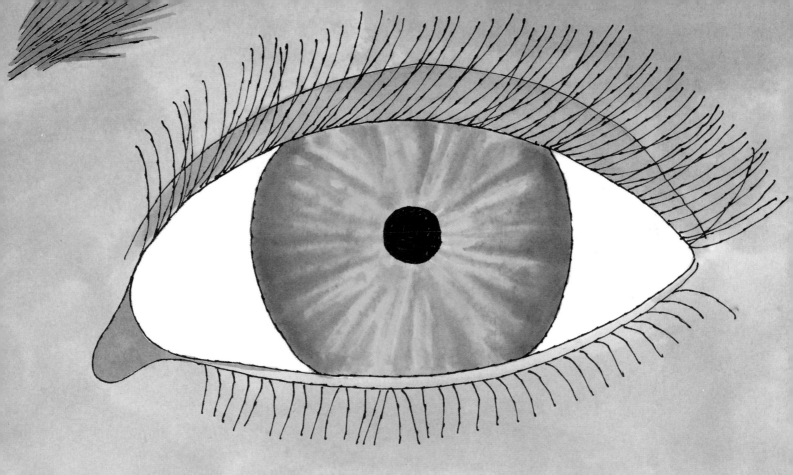

When you look at your eyes, you see a black spot in the middle of each one. The black spot is called the pupil. Sometimes it is small. Sometimes it grows big.

Did you ever watch the pupil in your eye change its size?
Aunt Ruth showed me how to do it.

Stand in front of the mirror and close your eyes almost all
the way. Keep them open just a little
so you can see. Count to ten.

1 ··· 2 ··· 3 ··· 4 ··· 5 ··· 6 ···

One. Two. Three. Count up to ten.

Now open your eyes a little bit more.
Watch one of the pupils in the mirror.

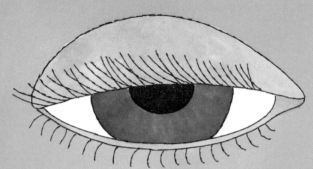

Open your eyes even more.
The pupil gets smaller.

Open your eyes up wide.
The pupil gets even smaller.

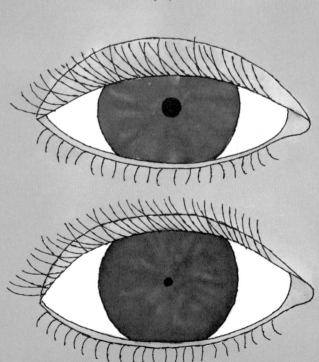

Why does the pupil change its size? Aunt Ruth says the pupil is a little round window. It lets the light into your eye.

Too much light can make your eye hurt. When the light is strong, the pupil gets small. It keeps out light that might hurt your eye.

At the beach the light is very bright. The pupils get very small, and you have to squint a little to help them protect your eyes.

At night or in a dark room, the pupil works the other way. It gets big. You need light to see by. The pupil gets big to let in every bit of light.

I like to look in the mirror. It's fun to look at my eyes and make faces. Sometimes I take too long. Then I hear my mother's voice.

"All right, all right," she calls to me. "Let's get a move on." Her voice sounds cross.

But when I come to breakfast, I can see she isn't cross because her eyes are smiling at me.